SESSION 1

BREATHTAKING BAY

Jesus is God's Son

Mark 1:1, 16-24

BREATHTAKING
BAY

I like these things best:

Chocolate bar ....

Sport ....

Movie ....

Toy ....

Animal ....

School subject ....

Hobby ....

In my family, there is...

If I were on a desert island I would take:

1

2

3

One word to describe me is...

ALL ABOUT ME

....

Mark 1:1
Jesus is God's Son. He is King of everything.

Mark 1:16-20
Jesus has power in his words.

Mark 1:21-28
Jesus has power over evil.

Mark 1:29-34
Jesus has power over sickness.

Who is Jesus?

1. **What did Simon, Andrew, James and John do, and why was it surprising?**

   (See Mark 1:18 and 20.)

2. **How else did Jesus show he was more than an ordinary man?**

3. Which of these events in Mark 1 do you find the most amazing? Why?

4. Do you think Jesus has just as much power and authority today? Why?

5. What do you think these events have to do with us?

The people wanted to find Jesus. Follow the path to Simon's house, and then to the hillside where Jesus was:

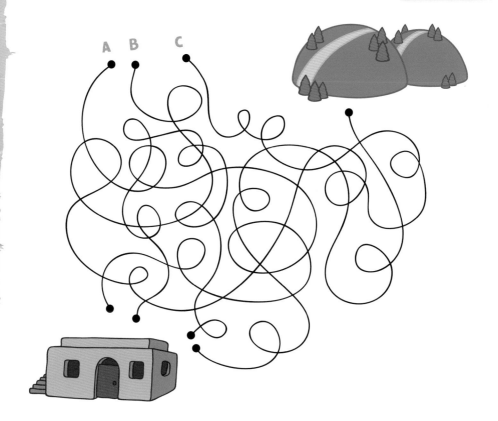

Cross out every green letter to work out people's reaction to Jesus.

PEAOPSLED   WEFREG   AMHAZJEDK   ATL

_ _ _ _ _ _   _ _ _ _   _ _ _ _ _ _   _ _ _

JEQSUWS'   PEOWRER   TANYD   AUUTIHOPRIOTY

_ _ _ _ _ '   _ _ _ _ _   _ _ _   _ _ _ _ _ _ _ _ _

7

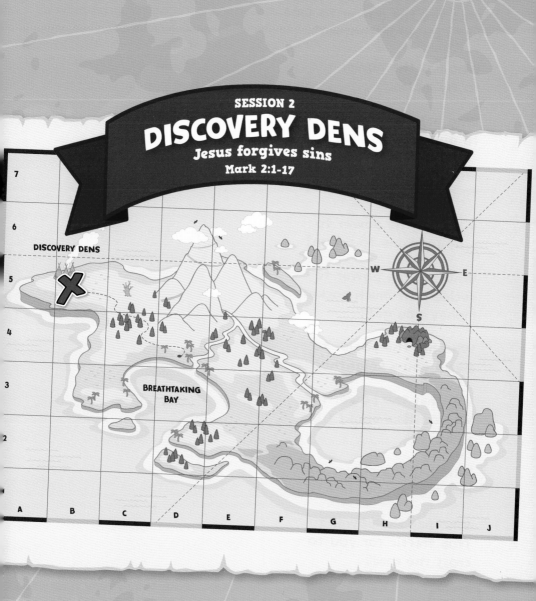

SESSION 2

DISCOVERY DENS
Jesus forgives sins
Mark 2:1-17

DISCOVERY DENS

BREATHTAKING
BAY

Who has the power to send
off a player in football?

....

Who has the power
to fly a plane?

....

Who has the power
to give you a filling?

....

Who has the power
to give you homework?

....

Who has the power to
send someone to prison?

....

Who has the power to
decide how much pocket
money you get?

....

Who has the power to
award you a knighthood?

....

Who has the power to
let you take books from
a library?

....

Who has the power to
operate on your heart?

....

Who has the power to
stop traffic for you to
cross the road?

....

WHO HAS THE POWER?

Mark 2:1-12
Jesus can forgive sin.

Mark 2:13-17
Jesus sees sin as our biggest problem and only he can deal with it.

Sin is when we don't treat God the way we should. It should be punished.

Why is sin such a problem?

1. **Brainstorm some of the different feelings experienced by the paralyzed man and his friends in Mark 2:1-12.**

2. **Why do you think Jesus forgives the man first?**

   (Have another look at Mark 2:17.)

3. Have a go at writing your own definition of the word "sin".

Sin is...

....

....

....

4. Do you think sin is a problem?

☐ Sin isn't a problem.

☐ God should let us off every time we do something wrong.

☐ Sin spoils our world and should be punished.

☐ Something else...

....

5. Can you think of ways you mess up or put yourself first? For example: cheat, lose your temper, etc. How would you feel if everyone could see all your wrong thoughts, words and actions?

Spot the difference between these two pictures of the healed man:

There are **5** differences to find.

Unscramble the letters to work out why Jesus came.

Jesus came to rescue us from the...

_ _ _ _ _ _ _ _ _

SESSION 3
MYSTERIOUS MOUNTAINS
Jesus died in our place
Mark 15

DISCOVERY DENS

MYSTERIOUS
MOUNTAINS

BREATHTAKING
BAY

WHO WEARS THESE HATS?

Mark 8:31
Jesus' death was planned.

Mark 15:22-39
Jesus died to take the punishment we deserve. He died in our place.

Mark 15:22-39
Jesus died so that we can be God's forgiven friends.

Why did Jesus have to die?

1. **What was surprising about what happened to Jesus in Mark 15? So why was Jesus not surprised?**

2. **What things do we think, say and do that deserve God's punishment?**

3. How would you feel if someone else deliberately took the punishment for something you had done?

☐ Smug - they're a fool for taking the blame.

☐ Guilty - I should have been punished instead.

☐ Bad - for the person who suffered.

☐ Grateful - thankful for the person who took my punishment.

☐ Or a mix of these?

4. What brilliant things will happen when Jesus takes the punishment for someone's sins?

....

....

....

5. Which of the reactions to Jesus' death is most like your own? Why?

☐ The confused crowd - you don't understand.

☐ The religious leaders - you don't need Jesus' help.

☐ The Roman soldier - wow! Jesus must be God!

Can you solve the crossword?

ACROSS

2. The _____ gambled for Jesus' clothes.
   Mark 15:16, 24

5. The crowd shouted that Pilate should _____
   Jesus. Mark 15:13

6. There was a notice written above Jesus that read:
   The _____ of the Jews. Mark 15:26

7. Jesus died in the place of _____ .
   Mark 15:15

8. "He _____ others but he can't save himself!"
   Mark 15:31

9. _____ criminals were killed either side of Jesus.
   Mark 15:27

DOWN

1. Jesus cried: "My ____, my ____, why have you forsaken me?" Mark 15:34

3. In the middle of the day, the sky went _____ .
   Mark 15:33

4. The Roman centurion said: "Surely this man was the ____ of God!" Mark 15:39

5. The temple _____ tore in two. Mark 15:38

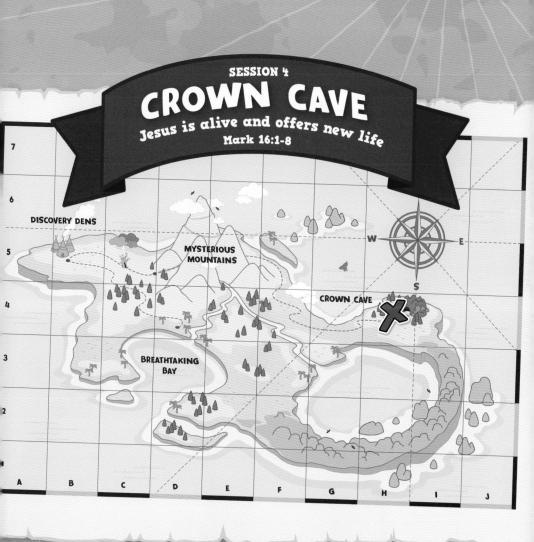

SESSION 4

CROWN CAVE
Jesus is alive and offers new life
Mark 16:1-8

Can you spot all the differences?

SPOT THE DIFFERENCE

Mark 15:42-47
Jesus definitely died.

Mark 16:1-8
Jesus definitely rose again.

In beating death, Jesus shows us that he is God and that we can have new life through him.

He has risen! He is not here.

Why does it matter that Jesus is alive?

1. **How do we know Jesus was definitely dead?** (see Mark 15:42-47.)

2. **What were the different things the women saw and heard when they arrived at the tomb** (Mark 16:4-6)**? Can you think of any other evidence that showed that Jesus was alive?**

3. **Should the women have been surprised that Jesus rose from the dead?**

(Look at Mark 16:7 and then Mark 8:31.)

4. **Do you believe that Jesus died and came to life? Draw a stick man on the scale...**

I don't believe ANY of it!	I think a lot of it is made up.	I think some of it is true but I'm not sure about all of it.	I think most of it is true but I have a few questions.	I believe ALL of it!

5. **Why is it important that Jesus rose again? Or isn't it?**

Can you find all these words in the wordsearch?

Afraid
Anoint
Body
Crucified
Disciples
Jesus
Mary
Risen
Rolled
Spices
Stone
Sunrise
Tomb

D	Q	B	N	Q	U	A	S	I	D	N	A	O	H	C
I	Z	Q	O	T	F	S	W	E	E	K	L	J	J	O
S	I	D	M	D	B	H	I	U	g	T	M	O	C	Z
C	U	U	X	A	Y	F	N	Y	J	E	S	U	S	T
I	V	M	L	K	I	V	W	D	F	N	I	Y	N	E
P	S	P	I	C	E	S	I	M	A	R	Y	I	S	F
L	O	F	U	U	J	A	W	E	C	Z	O	I	E	E
E	Q	R	F	V	R	H	N	N	S	N	R	F	P	X
S	C	Y	A	F	Z	O	H	U	A	N	B	I	I	P
A	Q	R	A	B	T	U	I	S	U	A	M	R	C	L
A	H	g	I	S	N	R	Z	S	R	U	g	S	F	O
T	Q	g	Y	S	g	H	O	F	Y	Z	N	T	P	R
B	O	T	T	J	E	T	D	R	O	L	L	E	D	E
P	E	M	V	B	O	N	L	A	V	T	L	A	J	R
L	W	N	B	E	D	N	Y	g	Y	B	O	T	J	S

Can you find all of these items hidden in the picture?

Butterfly
Horseshoe
Lemon
Snake

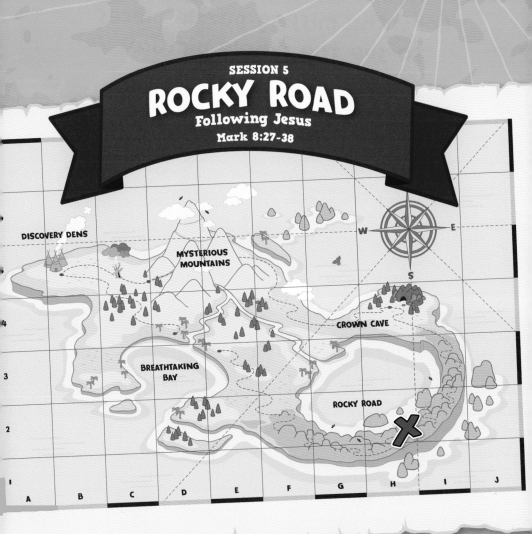

SESSION 5

ROCKY ROAD
Following Jesus
Mark 8:27-38

DISCOVERY DENS

MYSTERIOUS MOUNTAINS

CROWN CAVE

BREATHTAKING BAY

ROCKY ROAD

Copy the missing puzzle pieces to see the whole picture.

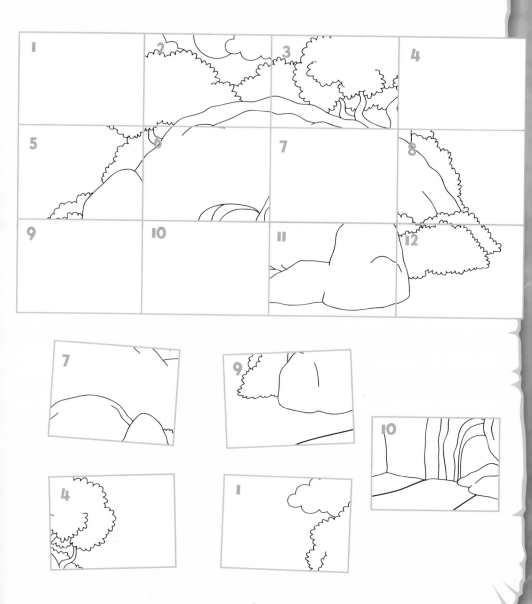

EXPLORER'S ENTRIES

Mark 8:29
Jesus is God's Son. He is King over everything.

Mark 8:31
Jesus had to die to provide the way for us to be forgiven.

Mark 8:34
If we love God, we should want to live his way even if it's hard.

What does it mean to follow Jesus?

1. What answer would you have given to Jesus' question: "Who am I?"

2. Which of these do you believe?

- [ ] I am a good person and hope I deserve to go to heaven.

- [ ] God will let me into heaven because I'm not that bad.

- [ ] I don't deserve it, but I can go to heaven because Jesus died to rescue me from my sin.

- [ ] I have done wrong and deserve to be punished by God.

3. How does the Bible say we can be accepted and forgiven by God?

4. "Being a Christian is just not worth it. You end up having no fun and having no friends. What's the point?"

Which bit of this statement seems true? Why do you want/not want to follow Jesus?

5. Do you have any questions about what it means to follow Jesus?

Take the first letter of each picture to discover something Jesus said about himself.

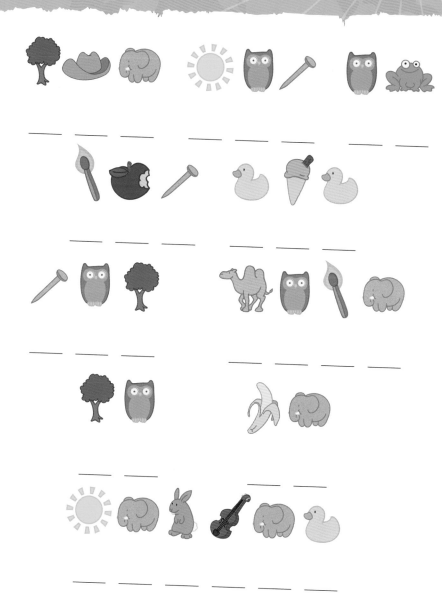

but to serve, and to give his life as a ransom for many.

Mark 10:45

CHRISTIANITY
EXPLORED
MINISTRIES

Epic Explorers Logbook
© Christianity Explored / The Good Book Company 2014.
Reprinted 2016.
www.ceministries.org

The Good Book Company
Tel: 0333 123 0880; International: +44 (0) 208 942 0880
Email: info@thegoodbook.co.uk

Websites
UK: www.thegoodbook.co.uk
North America: www.thegoodbook.com
Australia: www.thegoodbook.com.au
New Zealand: www.thegoodbook.co.nz

ISBN: 9781909919716

Illustration and cover design by André Parker
Design and layout by ninefootone creative / André Parker
Printed by Proost Industries NV. Belgium